PEOPLE OF
THE SOUTHWEST

by
LINDA THOMPSON

Rourke
Publishing LLC
Vero Beach, Florida 32964

www.rourkepublishing.com

PHOTO CREDITS:
Library of Congress, Prints & Photographs Division, Edward S. Curtis Collection: cover, title page, pages 4, 9, 11, 14-16, 21, 24, 27, 28, 31, 32, 37, 39, 40, 43; Courtesy of the Denver Public Library: page 11; Cliff Fragua and the New Mexico Statuary Commission: page 13; Cindy Hegger: pages 17, 30; Charles Reasoner: pages 20, 22; Courtesy of The Division of Anthropology, American Museum of Natural History (AMNH): pages 20, 34, 36-39, 41, 42; US Fish and Wildlife Service: page 14; Arizona Department of Tourism: page 26; Courtesy of the Library of Congress Prints and Photographs Division: page 34; Courtesy of the U.S. Marine Corps: page 43.

DESIGN AND LAYOUT by Rohm Padilla, Mi Casa Publications, printing@taosnet.com

Library of Congress Cataloging-In-Publication Data

Thompson, Linda, 1941-
  People of the Southwest / by Linda Thompson.
    p. cm. -- (Native peoples, Native lands)
Includes bibliographical references and index.
Contents: The southwest people today -- Where they came from -- Life in the southwest -- What they believe.
  ISBN 1-58952-760-7 (hardcover)
  1. Indians of North America--Southwest, New--History--Juvenile literature. 2. Indians of North America--Southwest, New--Social life and customs--Juvenile literature. [1. Indians of North America--Southwest, New.] I. Title. II. Series: Thompson, Linda, 1941- Native peoples, Native lands.
  E78.S7.T489 2003
  979.004'97--dc21
                                        2003011547

Printed in the U.S.A.

TITLE PAGE IMAGE
Apache-land; photo by Edward S. Curtis.
Apache horsewomen in a small valley of the White Mountain region. The horses are laden with the complete camp equipment, on top of which the women have taken their seats.

TABLE OF CONTENTS

Rocks against the
sky in New Mexico

Chapter I:

THE SOUTHWEST PEOPLE

More than 50 **Native American** tribes (sometimes called **American Indians**) once lived in the region that is now the U.S. Southwest. This region includes the states of New Mexico and Arizona, and small pieces of southern California, Utah, and Colorado.

This country is dry, with average rainfall below 20 inches (51 cm) a year. Much of the land is high desert, 5,000 to 8,000 feet (1,524 to 2,438 m) above sea level. Mountains soar to 13,000 feet (3,962 m) and higher. Temperatures can reach above 100° Fahrenheit (37.7° C) in summer, falling below freezing in winter. These conditions made life very challenging for early inhabitants.

The Gap at Walpi, Arizona

There may have been more than 200,000 **Southwest People** before European explorers and settlers arrived. Their languages came from a dozen major Native **language "families."** Today, about 320,000 descendants live in this region. Many tribes speak their original languages, as well as English.

NORTHWEST &
SUBARCTIC

C
A
L
I
F
O
R
N
I
A

PLATEAU

GREAT
BASIN

PLAINS

SOUTHWEST

NORTHEAST
WOODLANDS

SOUTHEAST
WOODLANDS

ATLANTIC
OCEAN

Two very different types of people occupied the Southwest–farmers and **nomadic** hunters. The early farming peoples lived near rivers such as the Colorado and Rio Grande, where they could more easily grow crops. Spanish explorers called these groups "pueblos" because they lived in permanent villages. The word "pueblo" means both "people" and "village."

SOUTHWEST

Hohokam flute player in the petroglyph style

About 600 years ago, Apache groups that for centuries had been moving south from Canada arrived in the Southwest. Different tribes claimed parts of the region, continuing their wanderings within those areas. Beginning about AD 1600, these nomads acquired horses, improving their ability to travel and hunt. Spaniards had introduced horses to America a century earlier.

The Apache called themselves **Tinneh** ("the people") but the Zuni named them **apacu** ("enemy"), which became "Apache." They traded meat and hides for food, cloth, and pottery at various pueblos. But the Apache also plundered the pueblos. They saw raiding as a normal extension of their hunter-gatherer lifestyle.

Sun petroglyphs from New Mexico

Knife from New Mexico made out of chipped basalt stone

The Southwest still has the remains of even older civilizations. Most Southwest farming tribes descended from three ancient peoples: the Hohokam, the Mogollon, and the Anasazi. They built villages out of stone, mud, and clay and etched or painted elaborate figures on rock faces. These **archaeological remains**, **pictographs,** and **petroglyphs** are well preserved because of the Southwest's very dry climate.

These ancient peoples grew corn, beans, and cotton. They developed irrigation systems to carry water to their crops. They made beautiful sculpture, baskets, pottery, and jewelry and traded with other Native Americans, including tribes throughout Mexico.

By the 14th century AD, these civilizations had disappeared. Nobody knows why, but long periods of **drought** seem to have been partly responsible. Their descendants include New Mexico's 19 pueblos, as well as tribes in Arizona. Some of the most famous Anasazi sites that still can be seen are **Mesa** Verde, Chaco Canyon, and Canyon de Chelly.

Kiva interior at Chaco Canyon's Pueblo Bonita

The invasion route of the Spanish came north through present day Mexico and continued throughout the Southwest.

Soon after Christopher Columbus "discovered" America in 1492, Spanish **conquistadors** defeated the Aztec empire in Mexico and the Inca empire in Peru. Those civilizations had great stores of gold and treasure, which Spain wanted. In about 1540, Spain began searching for additional treasure to the north. This search was about to bring major changes to the lives of Southwest Peoples.

A group of conquistadors led by Francisco Vasquez de Coronado came

Horses were first introduced to the Americas around AD 1500.

seeking legendary cities of gold, the "**Seven Cities of Cibola**." Rumors of golden cities "to the north" had come from Mexican Natives many years before. Coronado's troops arrived at Hawikuh Pueblo, in present-day New Mexico, where the Zuni lived. The Zuni had heard tales of these pale strangers dressed in metal and riding strange beasts (horses). Out of fear, they fought the Spaniards, but were overcome. Coronado fed his men from Zuni food stores. Speaking through Indians who came with him from Mexico, he assured the Zuni that he meant no further harm.

At the time of Coronado's visit, the pueblo world consisted of about 60,000 individuals living in more than 100 villages over 200,000 square miles (518,000 sq km). Although groups spoke different languages, the news of Coronado's arrival spread quickly. It was met with both fear and curiosity.

Coronado sent an expedition led by Captain Hernando de Alvarado to **Pekush** (Pecos), 200 miles (322 km) east of Zuni. On the way, they visited at least 80 pueblos, where they were welcomed. Because one of Spain's goals was to convert Native "savages" to Christianity, Franciscan **friars** accompanied the conquistadors. The friars **baptized** some Pueblo people and erected crosses on their lands. To the friars, this meant that the Natives had been converted. But the Natives did not have the same understanding. Because gift-giving was part of their culture, they possibly took the friars' actions as signs of friendship.

The Buffalo dance at Hano was introduced by the Hopi.

By AD 1600 Spaniards had colonized much of the Southwest.

But friendship was not the Spaniards' goal. Although he had promised no harm, that winter Coronado's troops killed 200 Natives at a complex of 12 pueblos called Tiguex, near where Albuquerque stands today. The Natives had resisted giving their homes, food, and blankets to his men. Coronado searched for more than two years and found no golden cities. He brought the Pueblo People only misery. Finally, he gave up and returned to Mexico, leaving the friars behind to continue their work.

In 1598, Juan de Oñate set up Spain's first permanent colony, San Gabriel, near the present San Juan Pueblo. In December, Oñate's nephew, Juan de Zaldívar, led an expedition toward Arizona, seeking gold. Cold and hungry, the Spaniards demanded provisions at Acoma Pueblo, west of present-day Albuquerque. The Acoma resisted, killing Zaldívar and several others. In revenge, a Spanish contingent from San Gabriel slaughtered 800 Natives. Male survivors were sentenced to have one foot cut off and to serve 20 years of slavery. The women were given to the Apache as slaves.

The first church at Taos Pueblo was destroyed in the revolt of 1680.

Native American Apache men pose with a bow and arrow, staff, and rifle.

Oñate ordered the Pueblos to give up blankets, food, and even their sacred corn seed. When rain failed for several years, both Natives and conquistadors began to starve. As the Spaniards kept seizing the Pueblos' food and goods, the vast trading network collapsed. This led to increased Apache raiding.

From the Spaniards, the Apache had acquired metal for spears and arrowheads, as well as many horses. Their raids became brutal. For protection, Pueblo People began to look to Christianity. By 1608, the friars had baptized 7,000 Natives. To serve these new converts, Spain built a capitol at Santa Fe. The conquistadors began planting crops, to be cultivated by Spanish soldier-settlers. Growing food meant that soldiers could stop seizing provisions from the pueblos.

Acoma Pueblo, New Mexico, with church at center. In the distance is Mount Taylor.

By 1620, there were 17,000 converted Natives. But the Pueblo People found Christianity foreign in many ways. They believed that people came from below the earth and returned there after they died. They could not comprehend a creator who lived up above. They continued in their old beliefs, adding some Christian ceremonies to their own.

The Zuni prayer symbol for the end of war shows two arrow points coming together.

At this time, the slave trade was very prosperous. Slaves were needed to mine silver in Mexico. The Spanish soldiers at first captured slaves from Apache and other Plains tribes. Later, the Apache sold Native prisoners to the Spanish. All of these Natives were roped together and marched in long columns to Mexico.

Landscape near Zuni Reservation, New Mexico

Diseases that the Spaniards brought wiped out thousands of Native people. By 1650, only about 50 pueblos were still occupied. Twenty years later, animal diseases, drought, and Apache raids had also eliminated most of the Natives' cattle, sheep, and pigs.

Conquistador, or "Conqueror" on horseback

Finally, anger turned into action. Guided by **shamans,** the Pueblos began rebelling. A medicine man named Popé led the Pueblo Revolt of 1680, which began in Taos. The Natives killed every Spanish soldier, priest, and settler they could find. They succeeded in driving the rest into Mexico. Popé and his followers tried to eliminate everything Spanish. But the drought and Apache raids continued. In a few years, only a few dozen New Mexico pueblos remained inhabited.

Sculpture of Pueblo Revolt leader Popé

Geronimo

Apache leaders in the 19th century included Mangas Colorado, Cochise, and Geronimo. During years of resistance, the Apache blocked stagecoach routes and fought both U.S. and Mexican forces. Goyahkla ("One Who Yawns"), an Eastern Chiricahua Apache, became a shaman as well as a chief. After his wife, children, and mother were murdered in a Mexican raid, he had a vision that said no gun could kill him. When he attacked the Mexicans, they screamed "Geromino," calling on their patron saint, St. Jerome. That name stuck, and Goyahkla became Geronimo.

Then, in 1692, the Spanish returned to Santa Fe. Ready for relief, many Pueblo people welcomed them, and eventually Spain regained control of New Mexico. Within a century, 20,000 Spanish immigrants had settled there. But Pueblo populations continued to shrink. The population of the Zuni, for example, fell from several thousand people in 1630 to only 200 by 1760.

The Hopi in northeastern Arizona were not as disrupted by the conquistadors. Their high, dry mesas were not attractive to settlers. It was not until the first U.S. Indian agent was appointed in 1870 that the Hopi began to feel the effects of the European expansion. In 1882, the U.S. established a **reservation** for the Hopi, which amounted to only a portion of their original **tutsqua**, or homeland.

Today, New Mexico Pueblo People live in 19 remaining pueblos, now recognized as individual reservations. They raise horses, mules, cattle, chickens, sheep, and goats. Although people have moved away, their sense of community is very strong. Individuals and families frequently return to celebrate major feast days and holidays in their pueblos.

The Apache story is different. By 1700, they had divided into seven groups, including the **Navajo**. The Navajo had changed their culture so much that they were no longer called Apache. The Lipan and Kiowa Apache resembled the Plains People in many ways and remained in the eastern part of the region. Four other groups chose territory along the Rio Grande. These were the Jicarilla and Mescalero tribes, who roamed the river's eastern edge, and the Chiricahua and Western Apache, who stayed west of the river.

The Apache were the last Native Americans to be confined on reservations.

Now, about 17,000 Apache live on or near four main reservations in Oklahoma, Arizona, and New Mexico.

Eskadi Apache, a headman for one of the bands

The Navajo (**Diné** or "the people") live in a large region around the Four Corners area, where the present states of Utah, Colorado, Arizona, and New Mexico meet. They call this ancient homeland **Diné Tah** ("Among the People"). Because they intermarried more with Pueblo People than other Apache did, they became experts in growing crops. From the Spanish, the Navajo acquired horses, cows, and sheep. By the 19th century, some Navajo families had become wealthy.

But by that time, European settlers wanted their land. Led by the famous "Indian fighter," Kit Carson, the U.S. Army rounded up more than 9,000 Navajo. They were marched to the **Bosque Redondo** ("round grove"), a reservation with bad water 300 miles (483 km) to the southeast. More than 2,000 people died from disease and starvation. In 1868, the Navajo were released and permitted to live on a portion of their former homeland. Although it is a fraction of their Diné Tah, their reservation is the largest in the country.

Cañon de Chelley in northeast Arizona

One thing that is very important to Natives on reservations is the concept of **sovereignty.** This means that people living on a reservation have their own laws and tribal organizations, and in many ways are not subject to U.S. or state laws. To Native Americans, sovereignty is not possession of the land but a living relationship between the people and the land that supports them.

In recent times, Natives have found new ways to make this relationship work. For instance, reservations have created **casinos** in states where gambling is otherwise illegal. The casinos create jobs and provide money for schools and other programs to raise the standard of living. In some areas, casinos employ non-Natives as well as Native residents.

Casino on Taos Pueblo reservation

Allan Houser (1914-1994) was born of Chiricahua Apache parents in Oklahoma. His father was captured with Geronimo. Allan became the most famous student of the Institute of American Indian Arts in Santa Fe. In sculpture, he said, "I found my soul." He produced nearly 1,000 sculptures in stone, wood, and bronze. Some of them are in the Metropolitan Museum of Art and other museums. In 1992, he was awarded the National Medal of Arts, the country's highest artistic honor.

Maria Martinez (1887-1980), and her husband, Julian, of San Ildefonso Pueblo, became famous for black-on-black pottery. In the 1920s, they tried to recreate the pots of their ancestors, of which only fragments remained. They invented a technique that gives some sections of the pots a **matte** finish and others a glossy black shine. Maria's son, Popovi Da (1921-1971) applied unusual designs to Maria's forms. Their pots are collected worldwide.

Pottery done in the black-on-black style

Wherever they live, Southwest People are engaged in preserving their heritage. They make baskets, drums, and pottery using traditional methods and continue to practice their religion. Young people study tribal languages, songs, dances, and ceremonies. They understand that learning these things will help keep their history and values alive.

The Southwest People have produced a number of individuals who have achieved recognition in art, music, film, writing, teaching, and other fields. By listening to their voices, Natives and non-Natives alike can better understand who the Southwest People were–and still are.

Chapter II

WHERE THEY CAME FROM

◄BERING STRAIT

Scientists believe that Native Americans descended from Asian people who walked across land or ice bridges beginning perhaps 30,000 years ago. Some may have come by boat. A land **migration** would have occurred at the Bering Strait, a narrow waterway between Siberia (a part of Russia) and the present state of Alaska. Sea levels might have been lower then, exposing land.

Within a few thousand years, descendants of these immigrants had spread across North, Central, and South America. They divided into hundreds of groups, speaking many languages. There is evidence that in some areas, they hunted **mammoths** and other large animals that are now extinct. Some groups lived as nomads, wandering great distances in search of food. If water was plentiful and they could grow food, they settled down. They used the materials around them to make tools and clothing, feed themselves, and build shelters.

Stone-pointed arrows were used for hunting.

The Southwest People have their own stories about how they originated. Most North American tribes believed that the first parents came either from underground or from the sky. Southwest tribes believe that spirits and people came from beneath the earth.

The Hopi say that there is a hole, known as a **sipapu** or **sipapuni**, at the bottom of the Grand Canyon. Through it, Earth dwellers emerged from the underworld in the very beginning. The Tewa-speaking people locate the sipapu in south-central Colorado, while the **Keres**-speaking tribes say it lies to the north. After death, they say, all beings will return to the underworld through the sipapu.

Illustration of Turquoise Boy, son of Changing Woman, from the Navajo legend. According to the story, he brought horses to the Navajo People.

The Mescalero Apache claim that Guadalupe Peak in Texas is the sacred entrance through which mountain spirits called **gans** emerged. The gans teach people how to live. The Apache searched for a homeland, helped by Twin War Gods, who destroy fearful monsters. The twins are the sons of Changing Woman. Spider Woman helped the Apache on their long journey.

The Navajo say that all creatures came from the underworld, emerging through a hollow reed. First Man and First Woman lived in the Diné Tah near a sacred mountain. They created the sun from a turquoise disk and the moon from a rock crystal. At dawn, they found a baby and raised it with help from spirits. The baby grew up and became Changing Woman, who created the Navajo from cornmeal and bits of her own skin.

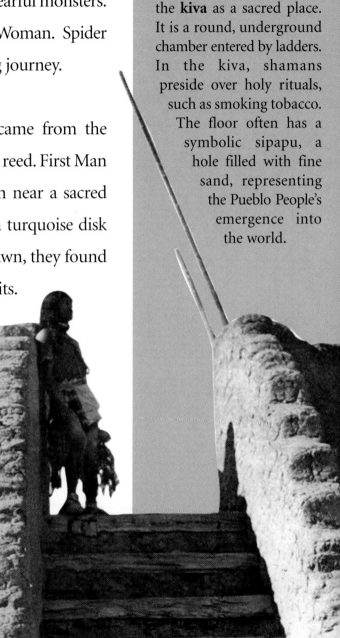

Zuni sun symbol

Early Pueblo People built the **kiva** as a sacred place. It is a round, underground chamber entered by ladders. In the kiva, shamans preside over holy rituals, such as smoking tobacco. The floor often has a symbolic sipapu, a hole filled with fine sand, representing the Pueblo People's emergence into the world.

Tortoise-shell rattles were used in ceremonial dances.

The Hualapai, a Colorado River group, believed that the Great Spirit made humans out of the reeds that grow by the river. For the Yavapai, a related group in Arizona's Red Rock Mountains, Sun and Cloud embraced First Woman, producing the human race.

The Yuma say that Kokomaht, the Creator, lived beneath waters covering the world. From him came everything good, but only evil came from his blind twin, Bakotahl. They made land, people, trees, mountains, animals, and fish. Kokomaht made himself a son, Komashtam'ho. Leaving his son in charge, he died so that people would not live forever and crowd the Earth. Komashtam'ho turned himself into four eagles that watch over the Yuma. Bakotahl lives beneath the earth. When he rolls over, it causes earthquakes, volcanoes, fires, and storms.

The eagle plays a major part in Native American spirituality.

The creation stories told by a tribe or a nation attempt to explain how people and everything else on Earth came into existence. These are just a few among the countless tales that the Southwest People pass from generation to generation to make sure that their history, ancient knowledge, and culture survive.

Ruins of community house
at Bandelier, New Mexico

Chapter III:
LIFE IN THE SOUTHWEST

*T*he Pueblo Peoples built their homes out of rock and clay or carved them into the earth. The abundance of relatively soft materials such as **adobe** and **sandstone** made it easy to build underground structures and caves in rock walls. Such openings in the earth represent doors into the sacred underworld.

Villages such as Taos and Acoma are aboveground. The stone and adobe walls absorb the sun's heat during the day, releasing it into the rooms at night. Rooms are stacked in tiers, so that each roof is a balcony for the home above. The balconies are used for everything from storing wood to cooking in **hornos** (clay ovens).

Feast Day at Acoma Pueblo, New Mexico

Originally, each family lived in a single room, entered by a ladder through a hole in the roof. Furnishings were sparse. People might sit on a block of wood or a folded blanket. At night they wrapped up in blankets and furs and slept in a row. Now, homes are larger and have more furniture.

Corn was central as a food source and was ground and used in a variety of ways.

The first Pueblo People grew corn, pumpkins, melons, beans, and squash. They hunted deer, antelope, and small game. They adopted horses, cattle, and sheep, from the Spanish, along with wheat, grapes, peaches, and apples. They kept captive eagles and used their feathers in ceremonies.

Ladders were used in multistory pueblo buildings.

Traditional hornos (clay ovens)

Apache moccasins made from buckskin and decorated with beads

For centuries, Pueblo People raised cotton and wove it into cloth. They also made deerskin into tunics and leggings. When Europeans introduced sheep, they learned to spin wool for clothing. They crafted ornaments from shells and turquoise beads and later learned metal-working from the Spanish.

Corn was the most important food. Women ground dried kernels into flour to make at least 30 different dishes, from bread to mush. In addition, they ate pine nuts, onions, fruit of the **prickly pear** cactus, and other wild vegetables. They ate parts of the **yucca** plant, wove its leaves into rope, and made soap from its roots. Pueblo tribes used dozens of plants to heal illnesses. They carved clubs, bows, and arrows from wood and wove baskets from grasses and stems. They used all parts of an animal. Skins became drums and clothing, bones became tools, and hooves became rattles. Bowstrings were made from **sinews**.

Prickly Pear blossoms (left), will grow into a small pear size fruit (above) and provide a nourishing food source.

Apache wikiup made of grass-covered tree limbs

Before the Apache got horses, they attached poles to dogs for hauling their belongings from camp to camp. They settled down only for the winter, living in **wikiups**, cone-shaped dwellings made of tree limbs covered with grass or yucca leaves. The Eastern Apache, however, adopted the tipi of the Plains Indians.

The Apache who lived nearest the pueblos grew some crops, including corn. They roasted **mescal** crowns in pit ovens and pounded them into thin cakes. They hunted deer, antelope, and mountain sheep with arrows that sometimes were tipped with poison. The Apache were known all over the West for their skill on horseback. Women were famous for their woven baskets, smeared inside with pitch so they would hold water.

Navajo woman with woven basket

The early Navajo moved often, seeking wild plants and game. They lived in **hogans** made of poles covered thickly with earth. Navajo families planted crops in the early summer, then moved their families and sheep to higher ground. At harvest time, some would return to the fields, while others stayed with the flock. The women spun and dyed the wool and wove the cloth. The Navajo used blankets for clothing and bedding. They also made **serapes**, shawls in which they carried firewood, food, and even babies.

A Navajo hogan made of earth and wood

A Navajo woman works in the corn field with a child on her back.

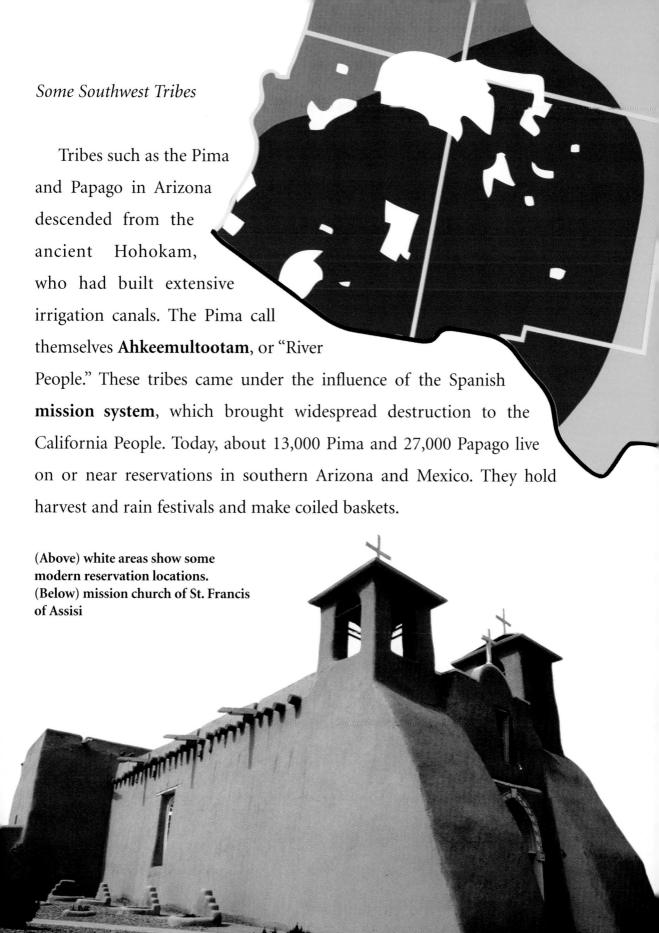

Some Southwest Tribes

Tribes such as the Pima and Papago in Arizona descended from the ancient Hohokam, who had built extensive irrigation canals. The Pima call themselves **Ahkeemultootam**, or "River People." These tribes came under the influence of the Spanish **mission system**, which brought widespread destruction to the California People. Today, about 13,000 Pima and 27,000 Papago live on or near reservations in southern Arizona and Mexico. They hold harvest and rain festivals and make coiled baskets.

**(Above) white areas show some modern reservation locations.
(Below) mission church of St. Francis of Assisi**

The Havasupai, or "People of the Blue-green Water," lived along the Colorado River, in the bottom of the Grand Canyon. Now, about 500 descendants live in nearby Havasu Canyon.

Hopi symbol for the sun

The Hopi speak a **Shoshone** language called **Uto-Aztecan**. The 1.6-million-acre (.65 million ha) Hopi Indian Reservation, established in 1882, is in the center of the Navajo Reservation in Arizona. About 9,000 Hopi and 2,000 people of other tribes live on high mesas reaching out from Black Mesa. Of about 75 Hopi clans, only 34 remain.

The terrain along some parts of the Rio Grande is similar to the Grand Canyon.

There are about 8,000 Zuni today. They are descended from the ancient Mogollon People and have their own language. Most Zuni live on a 400,000-acre (161,880-ha) reservation on the western edge of New Mexico. They grow 17 kinds of corn. They build houses from local stone and mortar, plastered and painted with whitewash. Today, modern materials such as concrete block are also used.

The Acoma and Laguna Pueblo People speak Keres-related languages. Laguna, on the San José River, has some 7,000 people. Acoma, west of Albuquerque, sits on a 357-foot (109 m) high mesa. It is now mostly used for ceremonies and tours, with most of the 4,000 people living below the mesa.

The old well at Acoma, New Mexico

Blue Lake, the source of Taos People's drinking water, is a holy shrine. The Taos used to bathe there and pray for a successful hunt. In 1906, the U.S. government took Blue Lake away. Soon non-Natives were cutting trees, bringing in cattle, and removing prayer sticks and other offerings. The Taos asked the government to return their sacred land. Finally, in 1970, the Senate voted to return Blue Lake and 48,000 acres (19,425 ha) of forest to the Taos Pueblo. It was a rare case in which Native Americans succeeded in regaining their ancestral lands.

The **Tanoan**-speaking pueblos are mostly along the Rio Grande between Albuquerque and Taos. Tanoan is divided into three languages: Tiwa, Tewa, and Towa. The Taos and Picuris People speak Tiwa. San Juan and Santa Clara are two of the Tewa-speaking Pueblos. Jemez People speak Towa.

Willow, a native of Taos Pueblo, dressed in traditional attire

Taos Pueblo looks much as it did when Coronado first saw it in 1540. It has been named a United Nations World Heritage Site. By law, the 700-year-old village has no electricity, running water, or indoor plumbing. About 1,500 people live there, and others live nearby.

About 17,000 Apache live on several reservations. The largest are Fort Apache in Arizona and the Jicarilla and Mescalero reservations in New Mexico. In addition, about 500 Apache live at the Anadarko Agency in Oklahoma.

Present-day Taos Pueblo

Navajo woven blanket

Navajo necklace
made of silver
and turquoise

The Navajo are the largest North American Indian tribe. More than 200,000 people live on a reservation that is half the size of England. It stretches across the northwest corner of New Mexico and a large piece of northeast Arizona. The Navajo learned silversmithing from Mexicans and developed their own Indian designs. They originally learned both weaving and **sand painting** from Pueblo people. Today, the Navajo are especially famous for their beautiful blankets, rugs, and serapes.

Sand paintings take days to produce and are destroyed after the ceremony.

Chapter IV:
WHAT THEY BELIEVE

*A*ll Native peoples' calendars, religion, and legends are based on nature. Their lives still revolve around their relationship with the earth. To them, everything has a spiritual purpose and is interconnected. Although they may have adapted to new ways and new religions, the old faith remains alive and is evident in their teachings, writings, art, and culture.

Southwest Peoples see spirit beings as part of the natural world. Their ceremonies combine features of their ancient religions with those of Christianity. Southwest Peoples' art, including paintings, sculpture, baskets, blankets, pottery, and sand paintings, express their feelings about the land and the forces within it.

Ladder leading to a cave dwelling at Bandelier, New Mexico

Saalako, a female Hopi Kachina doll

Corn is sacred to many Native Americans, and especially to Southwest People. It represents the link between humans and the spirit world.

The Hopi say that when they emerged from the Third World into the Fourth World, different peoples were given ears of corn. The Hopi got the shortest ear of blue corn, meaning that life in the Fourth World would be hard for them. A valuable lesson has come from cultivating corn over the centuries. It has taught the Hopi humility, cooperation, respect, and how to care for the earth.

The Pueblo People dance the Corn Dance every summer to express their gratitude for corn and to bless the season's crop.

Some Pueblo People believe in beings called **kachinas**. According to legend, they first taught humans to farm and hunt and communicate with the spirits. An important lesson was the need to cooperate with each other. In Pueblo culture, the group is more important than the individual.

Hopi Kachina doll

36

It is said that the kachinas come from underground to spend part of each year with the Pueblo People. Small painted dolls in their images are carved out of cottonwood and kept as reminders of their presence. Also, masked dancers dressed as kachinas perform during ceremonies. The dances are said to be moving prayers. The Hopi call these spirits **katsinum**.

Hopi ceremonial rattle made from a gourd

Pueblo religious practices are private. Recording them with cameras or other means is not permitted. But visitors are welcome at many Pueblo festivals. Turtle, Buffalo, and Deer dances are commonly held during the winter, and the Corn Dance takes place in summer. These celebrations involve drumming, dancing, chanting, and feasting.

Shrines on Navajo land marked an event or boundary.

Many Native Americans believe in the "sacred hoop" or circle of life, sometimes called the "medicine wheel." This circle has the four directions–north, south, east, and west. These four directions are important to how people live and believe. In Pueblo rituals, the directions of "above" and "below" are often added.

Each of the directions has a symbolic meaning. The Navajo build their hogans with the entrance to the east. Visitors sit in the west. Zuni "prayer bowls," made of fired clay, have four raised corners to represent the four directions.

In the Southwest, mountains often are visible on all four horizons. Four sacred mountains surround the Navajo Diné Hah. They are Hesperus Peak on the north, Mount Taylor on the south, the San Francisco Peaks on the west, and Blanca Peak to the east. These mountains are in Arizona, Colorado, and New Mexico.

Zuni prayer bowl with four raised corners that represent the four sacred directions

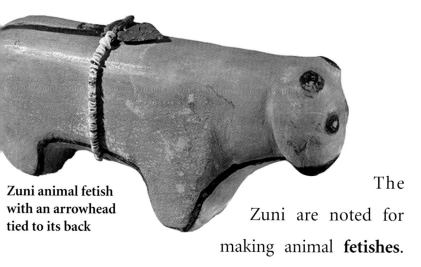

Zuni animal fetish with an arrowhead tied to its back

The Zuni are noted for making animal **fetishes**. These small charms, carved from wood or stone, have secret meanings. The Zuni believe that animals are closer to the gods than people. Some of the animals are guardians and promote healing.

A Zuni ceremony tells the story of their migration after emerging onto Earth. Dancers dressed as 10-foot (3 m) tall **Shalakos** (messengers of the rain gods) dance all night. At sunrise, they are sprinkled with sacred cornmeal and deposit prayer sticks asking for the village's happiness and prosperity.

Painted sticks with feathers attached by cotton cords were left in various sacred places, particularly in springs and at shrines, as offerings to the spirits associated with the locality.

The Apache felt that their actions and the power of the universe were closely related. For example, they would never plant corn in a field that had been struck by lightning. Before a hunt, the Apache purified themselves with sweat baths, fasting, and prayers. Neither women nor baskets were allowed on hunts for fear they would bring bad luck.

The Navajo have sacred ceremonies to relieve pain, cure illness, ensure good crops, and maintain harmony (**hózhó**) in the universe. Sacred singers (**ha'athali**) perform chants. Frequently, the Navajo perform a ceremony called "The Blessingway" to celebrate important events and bring good fortune.

Offering to the sun at San Ildefonso, New Mexico

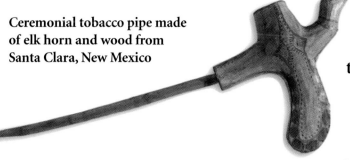

Native peoples once used **tobacco** as a sacred ceremonial plant. In tobacco ceremonies, smoke is considered a type of prayer. Hunters may smoke a pipe together to show respect for the animals that have died to feed them. The sacred uses of tobacco differ, but Southwest Peoples agree that tobacco should be used for prayer, protection, respect, and healing.

Native Americans were early **ecologists**–people who study relationships between **organisms** and their environment. Natives have always been dedicated to conserving nature, recycling resources, and ensuring a healthy world for future generations. In their view, humans are a part of nature, not a superior creature meant to dominate it.

Buffalo were a major natural resource for Native people.

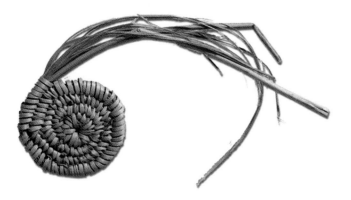

(Above) the beginning of a Navajo basket made from straw. (Below) the finished product had the inside coated with sap so it would hold water.

For example, the Hopi believe they have a sacred pact with **Massau**, guardian of the earth. As long as the Hopi care for the land as Massau has taught, they are allowed to remain in their homeland. Caring for the land is the underlying principle behind Hopi religion, culture, and daily life.

Badger paw design with prayer feathers in the palm of the hand

Taos Pueblo drum made from animal skin and wood

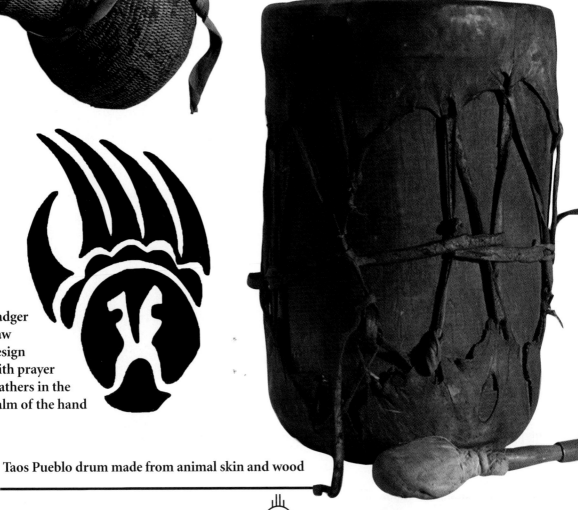

Native tribes' survival once depended on having strong, brave warriors. Ceremonies were held to honor warriors' deeds. Today, that feeling is maintained in the respect shown to veterans of U.S. wars. Large numbers of Native men and women have fought for the United States in every war. Powwows and tribal ceremonies often include flag songs and similar observances for Native veterans.

During World War II, the U.S. Marine Corps used Navajo recruits as "Code Talkers" to convey important messages among Marine planes, tanks, and battle stations in the Pacific. Their code, based on 211 Navajo words, turned out to be the only one that the Japanese could not break. Navajo words were given military meanings. For example, *gini*, which means "chicken hawk," was used to indicate "dive bomber." Eventually, about 400 Navajo served as Code Talkers. In 2002, a motion picture called *Windtalkers* told the story of these special veterans. Also in 2002, President Bush presented Congressional Gold Medals to the original 29 Code Talkers and Silver Medals to the others.

Geronimo

Navajo cousins from New Mexico relay orders over a field radio in the South Pacific, using their native tongue.

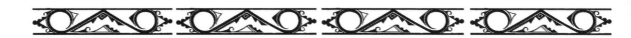

A TIMELINE OF THE HISTORY OF
THE SOUTHWEST PEOPLE

30,000 to 13,000 BC - Ice ages lower sea levels, making it possible for people to walk across a land bridge from Asia to North America.

12,000 to 9,000 BC - Earth warms up and the ice caps melt, allowing people to move throughout North, Central, and South America.

1,500 BC to AD 1300 - The Hohokam, the Mogollon, and the Anasazi build cities, and then begin to leave their settlements, probably because of drought.

AD 1300 to 1500 - The Pueblo People build more than 100 villages in the Rio Grande basin.

AD 1492 - Christopher Columbus arrives in America. Thinking he is in India, he names the inhabitants "Indians."

AD 1519 to 1531 - Spain conquers the Aztec Empire of Mexico and the Inca Empire of Peru

AD 1540 - Francisco Vasquez de Coronado arrives at Hawikuh, home of the Zuni.

AD 1500 to 1650 - Nomadic Apache tribes begin arriving in the Southwest.

AD 1598 - Juan de Oñate founds Spain's first permanent colony in the Southwest.

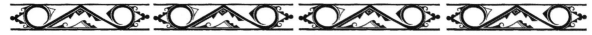

AD 1680 - Popé leads the Pueblo Revolt, forcing the Spanish from New Mexico until 1692, when they return.

AD 1776 - The American Revolution creates a new country, the United States of America.

AD 1804 to 1806 - The Lewis and Clark Expedition explores western lands from St. Louis to the mouth of the Columbia River.

AD 1821 - Mexico wins independence from Spain, making the Southwest Region part of Mexico.

AD 1846 to 1848 - Mexican troops attack General Zachary Taylor's forces and the U.S. declares war on Mexico. The Treaty of Guadalupe Hidalgo makes the Southwest Region part of the United States.

AD 1861 to 1865 - The American Civil War is fought and ends with the abolition of slavery.

AD 1882 - The United States establishes a reservation for the Hopi. In southern Arizona, the Yuman-speaking people, such as the Yavapai and Mohave, have been confined on reservations by the 1880s.

AD 1906 - United States takes the sacred Blue Lake from the Taos People and incorporates it into Carson National Forest.

AD 1970 - United States Senate returns Blue Lake to the Taos people.

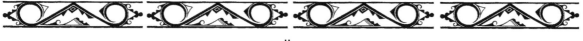

GLOSSARY

adobe - Bricks of sun-dried earth and straw.

Ahkeemultootam - "River People" in the Pima language.

American Indian - A member of the first peoples of North America.

apacu - Zuni word for "enemy," which later became "Apache."

archaeological remains - The traces of the culture of a people.

baptize - To initiate, purify, or give a name to someone.

Bosque Redondo - A place in New Mexico where the Navajo were confined in 1864.

casino - A building used for gambling.

conquistador - "conqueror." A leader in the Spanish conquest of America.

Diné - The Navajo name for themselves, meaning "the people."

Diné Tah - The Navajo name for their homeland, meaning "among the people."

drought - A long period of dryness.

ecologist - A scientist who studies the relationships between organisms and their environment.

fetish - Small stone or carving, believed to have magical power to protect or aid.

friar - A member of a religious order.

gans - Apache word for mountain spirits that help and teach their people.

ha'athali - Navajo name for singers who perform during sacred ceremonies.

hogan - Type of home built by the Navajo, originally made of logs and mud.

horno - Spanish word for "oven."

hózhó - Navajo word meaning "harmony in the universe."

kachina - Spirit beings, also refers to carved dolls made in their images and certain dancers at Pueblo ceremonies.

katsinum - Hopi word for kachinas.

Keres - Language family in the Rio Grande area.

kiva - An underground structure that Pueblo People use as a ceremonial chamber.

language family - A group of languages related to each other by similarities in vocabulary, grammar, and pronunciation.

mammoth - Extinct hairy elephants living about 1,600,000 years ago. They were several times larger than existing elephants.

Massau - Hopi name for the Guardian of the Earth or Great Spirit.

matte - A surface free of gloss; not shiny.

mesa - Spanish word for "table." An isolated, relatively flat-topped hill.

mescal - A type of cactus. The Apache and other Natives cooked mescal to eat and also brewed it into a liquor.

migration - The movement of a person or group from one place to another.

mission system - The main method Spain used to establish colonies in the Americas.

Native American - A synonym for American Indian.

Navajo - Probably from a Tewa word, navahu, meaning "arroyo with planted fields."

nomad, nomadic - Refers to people who move from place to place and have no fixed residence, usually in relation to the seasons and food supply.

organism - A living being.

Pekush - The original name of the New Mexico Pueblo now called "Pecos."

petroglyph - A prehistoric carving or inscription on a rock.

pictograph - A prehistoric drawing or painting on a rock.

prickly pear - Cactus with flat, spiny joints.

reservation - "Indian reservations" are the tracts that were set aside for Natives all across America and Canada.

sand painting - Symbolic pictures created in sand. The Pueblo Peoples painted sacred pictures on the floors of kivas.

sandstone - A rock made of sand particles (usually quartz) bound together with a natural cement such as silica.

serape - A woolen shawl worn over the shoulders.

Seven Cities of Cibola - A legendary place believed to have stores of gold and treasure, supposedly in the Southwest.

Shalakos - Supernatural figures, also, the people who dress as these figures and perform the Zuni Shalako Ceremony.

shaman - Medicine man or woman; a teacher and a healer wrapped into one.

Shoshone - Relating to a large, extensive language family, Shoshonean, also called Uto-Aztecan.

sinew - Fiber from tendons, the animal tissue that connects muscles.

sipapu - The hole from which humans emerged from the underworld to live on Earth. Also, the hole in the floor of a kiva.

Southwest People - The Natives of a region in the Southwestern U.S. and North Mexico.

sovereignty - Independent power and freedom from outside control.

Tanoan - A language family that includes several Pueblo languages and dialects.

Tinneh - Apache name for themselves, meaning "the people."

tobacco - A native American plant that belongs to the nightshade family.

tutsqua - Hopi word for "homeland."

Uto-Aztecan - A major language family of the Southwest, also known as Shoshonean.

wikiup - A kind of hut built by nomadic Natives that has sticks or canes for a frame and brush, grass, or bark for a covering.

yucca - A plant of the lily family native to the Southwest.

Books of Interest

Clark, Ann Nolan. *Sun Journey: A Story of Zuni Pueblo*. Santa Fe: Ancient City Press, 1988.

Erlich, Amy, adapter. *Wounded Knee: An Indian History of the American West*. New York: Henry Holt & Co. 1993 (adaptation for young readers of Dee Brown's *Bury My Heart at Wounded Knee*, Henry Holt & Co., 1970).

Erdoes, Richard and Alfonso Ortiz, eds. *American Indian Myths and Legends*. New York: Pantheon, 1984.

Hook, Jason. *Geronimo: Last Renegade of the Apache*. Dorset, UK: Firebird Books, Ltd., 1989.

Johnson, Michael. *Encyclopedia of Native Tribes of North America*. New York: Gramercy Books, 2001.

Keegan, M. K. *Enduring Culture: A Century of Photography of the Southwest Indians*. Santa Fe: Clear Light Publishers, 1990.

La Farge, Oliver. *The American Indian*. New York: Golden Press, 1956.

Liptak, Karen. *Indians of the Southwest*. New York, NY: Facts on File, 1991.

Nerburn, Kent, ed. *The Wisdom of the Native Americans*. Novato, Calif.: New World Library, 1999.

Vallo, Lawrence Jonathan. *Tales of a Pueblo Boy*. Santa Fe: Sunstone Press, 1987.

Velarde, Pablita. *Old Father Storyteller*. Santa Fe: Clear Light Publishers, 1989.

Warren, Scott. *Cities in the Sand: The Ancient Civilizations of the Southwest*. San Francisco: Chronicle Books, 1992.

Woodhead, Henry, series ed. *The American Indians*. Alexandria, Va.: Time Life Inc., 1992-94.

Children's Atlas of Native Americans. Chicago: Rand McNally & Co., 1996.

Good Web Sites to Begin Researching Native Americans

General Information Site with Links
http://www.nativeculture.com

Resources for Indigenous Cultures around the World
http://www.nativeweb.org/

Index of Native American Resources on the Internet
http://www.hanksville.org/NAresources/

News and Information from a Native American Perspective
http://www.indianz.com

An Online Newsletter Celebrating Native America
http://www.turtletrack.org

Native American History in the United States
http://web.uccs.edu/~history/index/nativeam.html

Internet School Library Media Center
http://falcon.jmu.edu/~ramseyil/native.htm

INDEX

Linda Thompson is a Montana native and a graduate of the University of Washington. She has been a teacher, writer, and editor in the San Francisco Bay Area for 30 years and now lives in Taos, New Mexico. She can be contacted through her web site, http://www.highmesaproductions.com

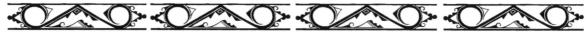